If Mama Ain't
Happy

By Averill Gardner Johnson

TRILOGY

If Mama Ain't Happy

Trilogy Christian Publishers A Wholly Owned Subsidiary of Trinity Broadcasting Network

2442 Michelle Drive Tustin, CA 92780

Copyright © 2021 by Averill Gardner Johnson

Rights Department, 2442 Michelle Drive, Tustin, CA 92780.

Trilogy Christian Publishing/TBN and colophon are trademarks of Trinity Broadcasting Network.

Cover design by: Natalee Dunning

For information about special discounts for bulk purchases, please contact Trilogy Christian Publishing.

Trilogy Disclaimer: The views and content expressed in this book are those of the author and may not necessarily reflect the views and doctrine of Trilogy Christian Publishing or the Trinity Broadcasting Network.

Manufactured in the United States of America

10 9 8 7 6 5 4 3 2 1

Library of Congress Cataloging-in-Publication Data is available.

ISBN: 978-1-63769-324-7

E-ISBN: 978-1-63769-325-4

This book is dedicated to:

My husband, Jeremiah. You are one of my favorite gifts from God. You are always so loving and supporting of all that God puts on my heart, especially this book. You have done so much to help this dream become a reality.

Our two boys, John Parker and Ezra. Because of you two, I have stepped into the biggest adventure of my life, being your Mama. I adore getting to watch you both grow in the Lord.

My parents, the greatest examples of living the Word of God continually that I have ever seen. You both have laid such a rock-solid foundation for me. I would not be where I am today without it.

My tribe of Mamas, my dearest friends that help keep me encouraged and keep my eyes focused on God's Word. Everyone needs friends like y'all!

Thank you all so much!

Table of Contents

Foreword

Averill Johnson has given every mommy a gift if they will open it. As I began to read, I yielded my thirty-seven years of parenting experience as I read *If Mama Ain't Happy* to this wise and lovely young mommy of two. In the most straightforward yet gentle way, Averill reminds us who we are and how important our role is, to our children, our family, our community, and most importantly, to the plans and purposes of God.

While normalizing the everyday things that can go wrong, she empowers moms with the Word of God to remind us of where our help comes from. Being a mom is no joke. My children's ages span twenty-seven years. The challenges of today are so much more in your face and the issues children faced in middle school they now encounter in elementary school! If you take your eyes off the Lord for a minute, you can have full-on panic at what is out there. But the Word of God, His promises, and His help will give us the courage and keep our children strong.

Yet, it is too easy to neglect that time with the Master every day. We know that it makes or breaks our day, yet somehow the day is spent before you get out of bed. Or so it seems. Averill has done us a great favor. She has done the study and written down the scriptures and encouragement that can start our day right.

We all need reminders of who we are and who we serve. Remembering the joys of raising a family when the "stuff" seems to overwhelm us keeps us in a place of gratitude and peace. We all need to keep our eyes keenly open to recognizing the attempts of the enemy to not only make us feel crazy but to find a foothold in our children's lives through our actions or inattentiveness to his tricks. I am happy to be able to recommend Averill's book to help in all these endeavors.

Jesus will partner with you to be a happy Mama with happy children. If you are reading this, then you are desirous to be the best mom you can be, be instant in season and out, to be the love of Jesus to your family and the thermostat in your home. I join Averill in cheering you on as you read. Let's all agree in faith for each other. Say this out loud, "I am the best mom my family could ever have! God has gifted my family by giving them me as a mom. I have His help every minute of every day. I am a happy Mama in Jesus' name!"

Read on,
Kellie Copeland

Introduction

I'm sure you have probably heard the phrase, "If Mama ain't happy, ain't nobody happy." I've heard it over the years. It is usually thrown around as a joke or just said to be funny, but to be honest, I've never really liked it. I feel like it makes Mamas seem moody, grumpy, and ill-tempered. As if one little thing doesn't go their way, they will take everyone down with them. But a few weeks ago, the Lord spoke to me about this and totally changed my perspective.

I was in the bathroom getting ready for church one morning, and the Lord started ever so gently speaking to my heart. He said, "Averill, you know the saying 'If Mama ain't happy, ain't nobody happy' is more than just a saying. It is a spiritual truth." Since then, He has taken me on a journey through His Word to see how beautiful the role of Mama really is, how, as Mamas, we help set the atmosphere of our home, and the specific things we can do to protect that atmosphere.

As I am writing this book, I have a few things I want you to understand:

1. I will be totally honest! I will bare my soul to you. There will probably be a couple of times that I will be too honest and give you too much information. I really don't mind as long as you get a laugh or are encouraged by it. I really believe that when we are completely open and honest is when we can really grow.

2. I do not want to ever give you just my opinion. My opinion, as much as I may like it, has never helped anyone. I do not

want to share anything with you that I cannot back up with God's Word.

3. I am a Bible translation connoisseur (a translation junkie might be more accurate, but connoisseur sounds classier). I have a really hard time sharing just one translation. I can't pick a favorite, so I might give you a lot of translations for some of the verses I share.

4. I am in no way a Mama expert, and I will never claim to be! I do not do things perfectly every time. I am still learning and growing. But I do know who is perfect—Jesus, and my purpose is always to point to Him!

I want to thank you for going on this journey with me. I pray that as you read this book, your perspective is changed, and you are encouraged, you laugh, you grow in Him and into the Mama He designed you to be.

Averill

Mama, We've All Been There, But Why Stay There?

◇◇◇◇◇◇◇◇◇◇◇◇◇◇

Being a Mama is the most amazing, beautiful, and rewarding job I have ever had. At the same time, it has also been the busiest, craziest, and most demanding job I have ever had. I used to work retail on Black Friday, and I'm telling you, that had nothing on the job of Mama! Being a Mama will require of you more hours, blood, sweat, and tears than any other job ever will, but I've never met a Mama that would trade it for anything. I know I sure wouldn't!

I remember both times we were at the hospital to have our boys. With each one, we were blessed with supernaturally fast and peaceful deliveries, but at the beginning of labor, I was honestly overwhelmed with all I knew was about to happen and how drastically our lives were changing.

I am a planner. I have stacks of notebooks, planners, pens, and highlighters, and I use them all! I make lists for everything, and I get super excited every time I can check something off. So, when it came to adding a baby to our family, I tackled that the same way. In preparation for the birth, I wrote lists, packed our vehicle, I laid out an outfit for both Jeremiah and myself, I put meals in the freezer, and did basically anything I could think of to make us more prepared. With both pregnancies, I

1

nested, prepped, and planned, but I still didn't really feel prepared. I'm sure in reality, no one ever feels ready.

With our first son, John Parker, I felt like I really had no
warning. My water broke at 3:30 in the morning, twelve days
before his due date. I woke up to the weirdest sensation I have
ever experienced. I was shocked, nervous, and excited all at
once. I sat up and said to my husband, "Jeremiah, my water
just broke!" Jeremiah rolled over, still half asleep, and started
to mumble, "Are you sure?" Then shot up, "Oh, never mind.
I feel it!" And just like that, we were on our way to the hospital
to have our first child.

Ezra coming into this world wasn't quite as dramatic, but
as labor started, I was a little anxious. This baby that had been
growing inside of me for the last nine months had to get out!
Thankfully, when anxiety tried to take over, we knew what to
do. By faith, we cast all of our cares on God, we spoke words
of faith instead of fear, and we played worship music in our
room. (Both times, we played my favorite worship album,
"Love Songs for the King" by Sarah Pearsons.) Both deliveries
were so supernatural and truly full of the presence of God.

I can still vividly remember each time they laid our babies
on my chest. I don't think any Mama can ever forget that
moment. The flood of emotions is so intense! The utter relief
that labor is over. Can all the Mamas give me an "Amen?" The
pure joy of holding our new baby, the thankfulness of being
blessed with such a sweet little one, the awe of finally getting
to see each one face to face. All these exciting new emotions,
but honestly, in the back of my mind, I was nervous and overwhelmed, thinking, *Okay, now I am responsible for another human*

being! This little one is totally dependent on me! I have to keep them alive and safe; I have to make sure they grow up happy and healthy!

I'm sure other Mamas can relate to me. Raising our children can be a very daunting task. No matter how old our children are, they will always be our babies. We will always have this driving desire to nurture, train, and care for them. The responsibility of this can be overwhelming. Trying to do it all constantly is truly too much for any Mama, but we are not supposed to do it by ourselves. It is when we try to do all this on our own that we find ourselves stressed out, worn out, and frustrated.

We've all been there! We've all had time where Mama ain't happy, and our families have known it. I'm sure I'm not the only one to have a "Mama meltdown." Our meltdowns may all look different, but they are still meltdowns. I'll be the first one to raise my hand and admit I've been there! I've let circumstances get to me. I've lost my cool and freaked out. I've cried, I've pouted, I've let my family know I'm upset. We've all had our moments, but just because we have all done, it does not mean it is supposed to be our normal. We've all been there, but why stay there? God has a better way!

> "I don't think the way you think. The way you work isn't the way I work." God's Decree. "For as the sky soars high above earth, so the way I work surpasses the way you work, and the way I think is beyond the way you think."
>
> Isaiah 55:8-9 (MSG)

If we let God be involved in our being a Mama, His ways will become our new normal. God's way of doing things is always better than our very best.

After all, who doesn't want that? God's way of doing things is far better than us in every area. That includes being the Mama He has called us to be! You see, He designed this beautiful position of Mama, and He has anointed you to fill it. He did not create it to stress or destroy you. He did not create it to have it wreak havoc in your family. He created you and your position in the family to bring peace, love, and laughter like you can.

The role of Mama is unlike any other role. It is a sacred role established by our Creator. It comes with many responsibilities spiritually, physically, and emotionally. We are supposed to love, train, nurture, protect, and comfort our children. From the first moment we hold our little one in our arms, we step into a role that is absolutely unlike any other.

I know that being a Mama and all it requires of us can seem so overwhelming, but God never designed us to do it on our own or in our own strength and abilities. We have Jesus Christ inside of us, empowering and equipping us to do *all* that is required of us.

> I can do all things [which He has called me to do] through Him who strengthens and empowers me [to fulfill His purpose—I am self-sufficient in Christ's sufficiency; I am ready for anything and equal to anything through Him who infuses me with inner strength and confident peace.]
>
> Philippians 4:13 (AMP)

Too many Mamas, myself included at times, are living stressed out because we are trying to fulfill this huge role all on our own. God never intended for us to do anything in life apart from Him. He wants in on everything, every part of our lives, the big and the small.

> The wise woman builds her house [on a foundation of godly precepts, and her household thrives], but the foolish one [who

lacks spiritual insight] tears it down with her own hands [by ignoring godly principles.]

Proverbs 14:1 (AMP)

This scripture sums up the entire heart of this book perfectly: living every part of our lives according to God's Word, including our role of Mama, and getting in on God's best in every area of our lives.

Mama, Our Role Is Important

The role of Mama is absolutely amazing. It is a truly beautiful position in the family lovingly created and placed there by God Himself. Mamas fill a place in the family that no one else can. We have been anointed by God to complete the role of Mama in our family.

Each Mama is unique. That is why we should never get sucked into the downward spiral of comparison. We have all been intricately, miraculously, and oh so wonderfully made by our Creator, specifically designed for each of our families.

"I will give thanks to you because I have been so amazingly and miraculously made. Your works are miraculous, and my soul is fully aware of this" (Psalm 139:14, GW).

"I thank you, God, for making me so mysteriously complex! Everything you do is marvelously breathtaking. It simply amazes me to think about it! How thoroughly you know me, Lord!" (Psalm 139:14, TPT).

Mysteriously complex and marvelously breathtaking. If that doesn't describe us Mamas I don't know what does! God has created each of us differently with unique callings, talents, and giftings. All of our lives look different, but beautifully so.

God absolutely adores diversity! That is why He made us all so different. He made us all uniquely special.

No matter how diverse we are, there are some things God has called all Mamas to do. And like anything else He desires for us, He has laid it out clearly in His Word.

> These words, which I am commanding you today, shall be [written] on your heart and mind. You shall teach them diligently to your children [impressing God's precepts on their minds and penetrating their hearts with His truths] and shall speak of them when you sit in your house and when you walk on the road and when you lie down and when you get up.
>
> Deuteronomy 6:6-7 (AMP)

Our greatest responsibility as a Mama is to fill our children and anyone in our home with the Word of God. We should not expect the church to be the one to fill our children with God's Word. If you are like me and have a church that is strong in the Lord and full of the Word, they do an amazing job of it, but we have so much more time with our family than they do. We have so many more opportunities to get the Word instilled in our children's hearts. We are the ones that build our children's foundation.

I know raising children to love and honor God in the world we live in today can seem overwhelming, but remember, God is bigger! The world is constantly trying to pull our children into its way of doing things, but the pull of God's Word is stronger if we plant it. God's Word cannot produce in our homes and families if we do not first plant it there.

The Lord spoke to me one day years ago and said, "You know there is a drastic difference between a 'Christian' home and a 'Word-filled' home." And that is so true! The label "Christian" has never saved anyone. Attending Church has never saved anyone. It is God's Word that is full of power. His Word is alive and can work in our families' lives if we let it.

"For the word of God is living and active and full of power [making it operative, energizing, and effective]" (Hebrews 4:12, AMP).

God has entrusted us with this huge responsibility of training and correcting our children in His ways. How we train and correct our children affects who our children grow into.

"Correct your child and one day you'll find he has changed and will bring you great delight" (Proverbs 29:17, TPT).

Correcting our children is not a one-time thing. It is a continual, daily process. It can be tough. It can feel like it is wearing you down but stick with it, Mama. It is so worth it! Having a child raised with no discipline is much worse than the process of disciplining a child as they grow.

"Pay close attention, my child, to your father's wise words and never forget your mother's instructions" (Proverbs 1:8, TPT).

"My son, obey your father's godly instruction and follow your mother's life-giving teaching" (Proverbs 6:20, TPT).

The most valuable, life-changing teachings we can ever give our families are the ones that point them to Jesus. Every day we have the opportunities to eternally impact our families for the kingdom. After all, in the end, it is what we have done for our families spiritually that truly matters.

"Train up a child in the way he should go [teaching him to seek God's wisdom and will for his abilities and talents], even when he is old he will not depart from it" (Proverbs 22:6, AMP).

"Train up a child in the way he should go [and in keeping with his individual gift or bent], and when he is old he will not depart from it" (Proverbs 22:6, AMPC).

That scripture shows us not only are we called to train all of our children in the ways of the Lord, but if we let God, He will show us special gifts and callings in our children individually that we can help cultivate and draw out of them.

We all know there is more to being a Mama than just giving birth to children. There are even Mamas that didn't give birth to their children but are amazing Mamas nonetheless. A Mama is one who loves, nurtures, cares for, disciplines, trains, comforts, and so much more. We could really talk on and on about all that Mamas do, but there is not a book big enough to really do the role justice.

The last chapter of Proverbs does a beautiful job of summing up the role of a godly wife and Mama. I know this is a long passage, so please bear with me. It is just all so good!

Who could ever find a wife like this one — she is a woman of strength and mighty valor!

She's full of wealth and wisdom. The price paid for her was greater than many jewels. Her husband has entrusted his heart to her, for she brings him the rich spoils of victory. All throughout her life, she brings him what is good and not evil. She searches out continually to possess that which is pure and righteous. She delights in the work of her hands. She gives out revelation-truth to feed others.

She is like a trading ship bringing divine supplies from the merchant. Even in the night season, she arises and sets food on the table for hungry ones in her house and for others. She sets her heart upon a nation and takes it as her own, carrying it within her. She labors there to plant the living vines.

She wraps herself in strength, might, and power in all her works. She tastes and experiences a better substance, and her shining light will not be extinguished, no matter how dark the night.

She stretches out her hands to help the needy, and she lays hold of the wheels of government.

She is known by her extravagant generosity to the poor, for she always reaches out her hands to those in need. She is not afraid of tribulation, for all her household is covered in dual garments of righteousness and grace. Her clothing is beautifully knit together—a purple gown of exquisite linen.

Her husband is famous and admired by all, sitting as the venerable judge of his people.

Even the works of righteousness she does for the benefit of her enemies. Bold power and glorious majesty are wrapped around her as she laughs with joy over the latter days. Her teachings are filled with wisdom and kindness as loving instruction pours from her lips. She watches over the ways of her household and meets every need they have. Her sons and daughters arise in one accord to extol her virtues, and her husband arises to speak of her in glowing terms. There are many valiant and noble ones, but you have ascended above them all! Charm can be misleading, and beauty is vain and so quickly fades, but this virtuous woman lives in the wonder, awe, and fear of the Lord. She will be praised throughout eternity. So, go ahead and give her the credit that is due, for she has become a radiant woman, and all of her loving works of righteousness deserves to be admired at the gateway of every city!

Proverbs 31:10-31 (TPT)

I know this sounds like such an extremely high standard. Being this kind of woman sounds completely impossible, but everything in God's Word does. It is all impossible on our own.

Don't let that overwhelm you. We were never designed to do any of it by ourselves. We have the Creator of the entire universe inside of us helping us to be the amazing Mama He has designed us to be.

"God is within her, she will not fall" (Psalm 46:5, NIV).

We will not fail at being the Mama God has called us to be as long as we do not try to do it all on our own. God has given His Word to guide us, His Holy Spirit to empower us, and His anointing to strengthen us.

"And I find that the strength of Christ's explosive power infuses me to conquer every difficulty" (Philippians 4:13, TPT).

In all that your families need from you, God has anointed and equipped you specifically for your family. No one can be the Mama for your children like you can. Mama, no one can fulfill your place in your family like you can.

Mama, We Are Influencers

◇◇◇◇◇◇◇◇◇◇◇◇◇◇

God has designed the position of Mama in such a way that we really do set the atmosphere in our home. Everyone in our family has their own amount of influence, but we Mamas seem to have more than any other family member. That is why "If Mama ain't happy, ain't nobody happy" is such a true statement.

Let's think about our personal experiences for a moment. If our child is upset or hurting, who do they want? Mama! I'm thirty years old now, and sometimes I still just want my Mama. There is something about hearing your Mama's voice and being wrapped in her arms that brings such comfort and peace. Even God compares the way He comforts His people to the way a Mama comforts her child.

"As a mother tenderly comforts her child, so will I tenderly comfort you..." (Isaiah 66:13, TPT)

Ideally, Mamas are supposed to have that peaceful, comforting effect, but that isn't always the case. If we are frustrated and full of strife, that breeds more frustration and strife in our homes. We can only influence our families with what is inside of us. That is why it is vital we stay full of God's Word.

If we are not happy, if we are not at peace, we will not create a happy, peaceful atmosphere in our homes. If we are not full of the Word, we cannot fill our homes with it. We cannot create an atmosphere around us that we do not first have going on inside of us.

The Bible shows us many examples of some truly amazing Mamas and the influence they had in their home and family. There are so many Mamas we could talk about, but I want to talk to you about my two absolute favorites. These Mamas in the Bible made a huge impact even though they only have a very small mention.

> As I think of your strong faith that was passed down through your family line. It began with your grandmother Lois, who passed it on to your dear mother, Eunice. And it's clear that you too are following in the footsteps of their godly example.
>
> 2 Timothy 1:5 (TPT)

Lois and Eunice were a grandmother and mother that used their God-given place of influence and made a huge impact. They are only in one Bible verse, but their influence was truly monumental. They raised Timothy. Because of their training and influence, he grew into a young man on fire for God. He became the pastor at Ephesus, led who knows how many people to the Lord, and had letters written to him that later became two books in the Bible. Today we are still being impacted by the investments these two ladies made, all because their love and passion for God influenced Timothy.

Every time I read this scripture, it makes me so thankful for the strong women God has placed in my life! I would not be where I am today if it weren't for their influences. I am who I am today because of them.

It is absolutely impossible to write a Bible-based book about Mamas and not talk about mine! In my eyes, she is the epitome of what a godly Mama should be. She loves her family big and loves Jesus even bigger. My mom is fiery and passionate for God. It is impossible to be around her and not get fired up. She has always held our family to the standard of God's Word.

While growing up, I sometimes thought she was the strictest mom ever, but as I matured, I began to understand she was just trying to protect us and the atmosphere in our home. My mom was just being a good steward over the children God had given her. She truly understood that children are a gift from God, and she honored and respected that gift.

"Children are a heritage from the LORD, offspring a reward from him" (Psalm 127:3-5, NIV).

Now I follow her example in every way possible. I am truly blessed to have a mom that I can follow as she follows Christ.

My grandmom, my dad's mom, is in heaven now, but she was such a sweet example of how to love your family and Jesus. She is where I inherited my love for cooking. She is also where I got my strong-willed personality. She was very determined and could not be talked out of something once she made up her mind. I know stubborn is probably the word for it, but that seems like such a negative word. It can be, but it really isn't if you are stubborn and refuse to be swayed about the right things.

One of my favorite stories I've heard about my grandmom took place shortly after she married my grandad. One evening my grandmom was cooking dinner, and my grandad came home from work. He had picked up a few things on the way home; one thing was a six-pack of beer (which seems absolutely outlandish now to me and anyone that knew him). My grandmom looked at him and asked, "What is this?" He answered her, "It's beer. I like one after dinner sometimes." She asked him to give them to her. When he did, she poured them all in the sink and emphatically stated, "That stuff will not come back in our house!" My grandaddy never had another drink. I always laugh any time I hear or tell this story. My grandmom was not a harsh person, but she was always adamant about sticking to godly morals.

My granny, my mom's mom, is still such a strong godly influence in our family. She is one of the most giving people I have ever met. As my mom was growing up, my granny instilled in her the value of going to church. She faithfully had my mom and her three brothers in church. Our family is still reaping a harvest of those seeds she planted in her children all those years ago. My granny and pappy even gave me my first Bible. She has also always been faithful to pray for each of us. Her sister, my great Aunt June, has also been a strong prayer warrior for me and my family.

I have so many godly women in my life that I could write a book just on them. So many that have loved and taught me. So many that have prayed for me. So many that have always pointed me to Jesus. No matter what is going on, they encourage me and always remind me what God's Word says. We all need to be surrounded with Mamas like that. Mamas that use their place of influence in our lives to build us up and draw us closer to Jesus.

We also need to be Mamas like that. We need to use our position of influence to draw those around us closer to Jesus. The future of our families and anyone around us depends on it—our influence matters.

What we do may seem small or insignificant to us some days, but we are making huge impacts. Every seed we plant in our children, husband, or anyone around us can grow into an eternal harvest. God's Word always grows and produces (Isaiah 55:6-11, NIV).

It is just up to us to plant it. We have to be so specific in what seeds we are planting. Good or bad, they will have a lasting impact.

We Mamas have this God-given ability to set the atmosphere in our homes and influence everyone in it. Whether we stay at home or work outside of it, we still set the atmosphere. We either use our position in the family to bring a supply of peace, love, and strength, or we use it to bring stress, strife, and division.

So Mama, let's decide today to make our homes a happy and peaceful one. Let's make the decision to use our place of influence in our family to impact them for God's kingdom.

Mama, We Cannot Give
What We Do Not Have

∞∞∞∞∞∞∞∞∞∞

I really cannot describe well enough how beautiful the job of Mama is, but as I said earlier, it is a calling that requires *a lot*! As Mamas, we are supposed to give love, comfort, strength, support, wisdom, etc. Our families look to us for so much, and many times we find ourselves stressed out because we feel like we just don't have enough to give them.

"I feel like I am just running on fumes." That is the phrase I have used many times to describe how I feel to my husband. Maybe Ezra was teething, so I was going on very little sleep, maybe I was volunteering at John Parker's school for multiple days in a row, maybe there were back to back events at our church, maybe we had Jeremiah's family visiting from out of town (my in-laws are absolutely amazing, but anytime you add extra people in the mix, schedules get crazy), or maybe that all happened in one week!

I know all of our schedules look different, but whatever your situation is, I'm sure you know exactly what I mean by "running on fumes." You feel like you have absolutely nothing left to give, not another ounce of energy or supply, but your family needs you.

No matter what is going on personally or what we feel like, we still have to take care of everyone. Feed them, wash clothes, clean the house, help with homework, and on top of all the natural things, we are still supposed to bring a spiritual supply to our family.

Have you ever had so much going on and been pulled in so many different directions that you didn't feel like you had any clue what you needed to do next? We have probably all accidentally put peanut butter in the freezer or gone into a room and had no idea why we went in there. We call it "Mom Brain." It is not that we are dumb; we are just extremely over-loaded. Well, I experienced a major "Mom Brain" moment a couple of nights ago.

Wednesday afternoons are usually pretty busy at our house. They are a mix of rushing to getting everyone ready for church, preparing to teach the youth group that night, and making sure everything is ready for work/school the next morning. Add all of that to our already busy household, and things can get pretty.

So, this past Wednesday evening, when Jeremiah got home, we were already running at full speed. I was washing dishes as he came in. At work, he is in the process of gutting and reno-vating a house, so he comes home pretty dirty. Before he went to shower, I asked him to throw his clothes into the washer, and I would start the load before we left for church. A little while later, I went into the laundry room. I added my pow-dered detergent to the washer, poured in the fabric softener, closed the door, and started one of the longest wash cycles I could pick. After church, I went to swap his work clothes over to the dryer, but the clothes in the dryer were still damp. So, I started the dryer again, and I just opened the washer door so his clothes wouldn't smell musty. Early the next morning, I took the clothes out of the dryer and went to get his clothes out of the washer. Y'all, the washer was empty! His clothes were about a foot from the washing machine, and I ran a completely empty washer! I had been so completely preoccupied that I didn't even see them.

This is just a funny example of what can happen when you have way too much going on. Well, it is funny now, but at the moment, it didn't seem funny at all. I was seriously overwhelmed and stressed out over a load of clothes. Being stretched too thin is never fun, and we can all eventually reach our breaking point. That morning, my breaking point was an empty washing machine.

I know we can all blame the stress, frustration, and burnout on not enough sleep, a hectic schedule, not enough "me time" to recoup, or a thousand other things. Needing those things is not bad, but they are never the root of our problem. The root is us trying to fulfill our role of Mama without Jesus.

"Yes, I am the vine; you are the branches. Those who remain in me, and I in them, will produce much fruit. For apart from me you can do nothing" (John 15:5, NLT).

"I am the Vine; You are the branches. Whoever lives in Me and I in him bears much (abundant) fruit. However, apart from Me [cut off from vital union with Me] you can do nothing" (John 15:4-5, AMPC).

Being able to do nothing apart from Him includes being the Mama we are called to be. We will not be able to train our children, comfort, nurture, or even love our family properly without our vital connection to Jesus. We cannot give our family something we do not have.

Make time for Jesus every day. Set aside time to read His Word. Set aside time to fellowship with Him through prayer. Set aside time to magnify Him through praise and worship. Set aside time to listen to Him; He is always speaking. We have to guard and protect our time with Jesus like our lives depend on it because they do!

The Bible is packed full of scriptures reminding us that we are strengthened in God's presence. I want to give you just a few of my favorites.

"Seek the Lord and His strength; yearn for and seek His face and to be in His presence continually" (1 Chronicles 16:11, AMPC).

"Depend on the Lord for strength. Always go to him for help" (1 Chronicles 16:11, ERV).

"He gives power to the tired and worn out, and strength to the weak" (Isaiah 40:29, TLB).

"But those who wait upon God get fresh strength. They spread their wings and soar like eagles, they run and don't get tired, they walk and don't lag behind" (Isaiah 40:31, MSG).

"But those who trust in the Lord will become strong again. They will be like eagles that grow new feathers. They will run and not get weak. They will walk and not get tired" (Isaiah 40:31, ERV).

"But those who wait for Yahweh's grace will experience divine strength. They will rise up on soaring wings and fly like eagles, run their race without growing weary, and walk through life without giving up" (Isaiah 40:31, TPT).

"Come to Me, all you who labor and are heavy-laden and overburdened, and I will cause you to rest. [I will ease and relieve and refresh your souls" (Matthew 11:28, AMPC).

"Are you weary, carrying a heavy burden? Then come to me. I will refresh your life, for I am your oasis" (Matthew 11:28-30, TPT).

Now, I know this last verse wasn't written just to Mamas, but I think it is probably one of the most fitting verses for us in the Bible. Being a Mama can really drain everything out of you physically, mentally, emotionally, and spiritually because we are constantly pouring into our family. That is why it is so vital that we spend time with Jesus every day to fill back up everything we have poured out to our families.

We could take all the vacations, all the spa days, and all the naps that the world could offer, but none of that can refresh and strengthen us like our time with Jesus can. A living, thriving, ongoing relationship with Him is the only thing that will satisfy us because that is what we were created for.

No matter how full our plate is, let's always make time for Jesus! Mama, let's get Him involved in every part of our lives, in every ounce of us, including our role of Mama. After all, this role in the family was designed by Him. He knows exactly what our family needs from us, and He alone is the source of it all.

When I was growing up, my mom was and still is the greatest example of this to me. I am the oldest of four kids, three girls and a boy. My sister Sarah and I are sixteen months apart, my sister Kristin and I are six years apart, and my brother James and I are thirteen years apart. So, for the last thirty years, my Mama has always had her hands full!

She and my dad have always done a phenomenal job of putting the Word first in our home. I have always seen them live what they preach. They are genuine. What everyone sees in the pulpit is what I grew up seeing at home, and I am forever grateful for that.

My Mama is honestly one of the busiest people I know. In thirty years, I have hardly seen her slow down. She always has a long to-do list, but I have never seen her forfeit her time with Jesus, no matter what is going on. She has always prioritized her time with Him. For as long as I can remember, my Mom has gotten up at five every morning to spend her time in the Word and pray for the family before everyone else gets up. She really had to because, once four kids are up, there is not a slow moment or a quiet spot in the entire house.

It has always been a running joke in our family that my mom never makes it through a movie. Every time we sat down to watch a movie, we would look over at my mom, and she would be asleep only a few minutes into it. It didn't matter how exciting the movie was or what time we started watching it, and she fell asleep.

I used to think it was so funny when she did that, and we would all tease her about it. But now I get up at five to read the Word and pray for my family, and now I am the one falling asleep during movies.

My mom is hardworking, dedicated, fiery, loving, kind, strong, and faithful. She has so many amazing traits that I desire to have, but the one I am most thankful to have picked up from her is her determination to always spend time with Jesus.

Luke 10:38-42 shares a story about two sisters that we are all pretty familiar with. Mary and Martha have been the source of many a sermon and many a Bible study and with good reason. They played out perfectly the decision we face every day to either get preoccupied with everything we have to do or spend time at Jesus' feet.

I feel like Martha has received kind of a bad rap. We all tend to look at her and think, *How could you choose cooking food over spending time with Jesus? He was right there in her house! What was she thinking?* But in all honesty, we have all done that at times. We have all chosen other things over our time with Jesus. We have all put off spending time at His feet because something else had our attention. Whenever we do that, we end up just like Martha, stressed out and frustrated.

Once I was reading their story when the Lord spoke to me. He said, "You know, Martha was not doing anything bad. She wanted to serve Me. Her only problem was she was trying to serve Me without first spending time at My feet. You can never serve Me properly without first spending time with Me." When Jesus spoke that to me, it completely changed my view on Martha. She and Mary both had the heart to serve Jesus, but Martha put the serving ahead of the relationship, and that never works. We will never be able to serve Jesus, our families, our church, or anyone else properly unless we are spending time at Jesus' feet.

As we spend our time with Jesus every day, we are giving Him the opportunity to impart into us everything our family needs, every encouraging word, every loving correction, every moment of comfort, and every piece of wise advice. The list could go on and on. When we are connected in daily fellowship with Jesus, our supply as a Mama is never-ending because our source is never-ending. Sometimes we Mamas can feel like we have so little to offer. Our families need so much from us, and we just do not feel like we have any more to give them.

But, if we will give Jesus the little we do have, He will multiply it just like the little boy's lunch (Matthew 14:13-21) and make it so much more than enough!

Mama, Happiness and Joy Are Not the Same

◇◇◇◇◇◇◇◇◇◇◇◇◇

I know the title of the book is *If Mama Ain't Happy*, but that phrase can actually be very misleading. Happy is an emotion, and, as we discussed earlier, emotions can change. Anything and everything can affect them. They can come and go depending on what is going on around us.

Happiness is a truly amazing emotion when we are experiencing it, but when it has faded, it can leave us very empty and let down. It's like coming off an emotional high. No one has the emotion of happiness all the time. Things happen that hurt us or bring sadness if we let them. You see, happiness is not constant, but joy is!

Joy is not an emotion; it is a fruit of the Spirit (Galatians 5:22). It does not come and go based on circumstances. Joy will continue to grow and produce in our life as long as we stay connected to the source, Jesus (John 15). Joy trumps happiness every time.

The Bible really has a lot to say about joy. As we study God's Word, we realize His view of joy might be different from ours. One of the reasons He gave us His Word is to change our perspective.

Joy is a source of strength that flows straight from our Father God.

"Don't be sad, because the joy from the Lord is your strength!" (Nehemiah 8:10, CEB)

The only place to get this joy is from the Lord. True joy is not available apart from Him. In His presence, we receive anything and everything we could ever need.

"In Your presence is fullness of joy"(Psalm 16:11, AMP)

"Being with you will fill me with joy" (Psalm 16:11, ICB)

Jesus is our unending source of joy. Our relationship with Him is where we get our joy.

"You love him passionately although you did not see him, but through believing in him you are saturated with an ecstatic joy, indescribably sublime and immersed in glory" (1 Peter 1:8, TPT).

Being truly happy, or more accurately full of joy, is not based on what is going on around us. It is based on what we have inside of us. It doesn't matter when things around us change. Jesus inside of us never changes.

"Jesus Christ is [eternally changeless, always] the same yesterday and today and forever" (Hebrews 13:8, AMP).

He is the foundation of our joy. He never changes. He never has an off day. Our joy never has to either.

One of my favorite examples of this is a ship. Think of a large cruise ship sailing in the middle of the ocean. That ship is completely surrounded by water, but no matter how much water is around it, it doesn't sink. The water around a ship will never sink it. It is the water that gets inside that sinks the ship. We are the same way. No matter what is going on around us, it cannot affect us unless we first let it inside of us.

It doesn't matter what is going on around us unless we let it matter. Joy is unmoved by circumstances. Joy is steadfast because it is grounded in Jesus. Joy will carry us through any trial or tribulation. We have joy not because we are excited about what is going on around us but because we are confident in who is inside of us.

"My fellow believers, when it seems as though you are facing nothing but difficulties see it as an invaluable opportunity to experience the greatest joy that you can!" (James 1:2, TPT)

Jesus has already defeated the devil and every power under him. He has made us more than conquerors. Jesus has already overcome whatever it is we are facing.

"Yet even in the midst of all these things, we triumph over them all, for God has made us to be more than conquerors, and his demonstrated loves is our glorious victory over everything!" (Romans 8:37, TPT)

"In the world you'll have trouble. But cheer up! I have defeated the world" (John 16:33, GW).

We already have the victory through Jesus. Just meditating on that could keep us joyful from now to eternity.

I want to add as a side note: surround yourself with friends that keep you laughing. Make your home an atmosphere that everyone can laugh in. Laughter is so needed. Even science has proven it is good for you.

"A joyful, cheerful heart brings healing to both body and soul. But the one whose heart is crushed struggles with sickness and depression" (Proverbs 17:22, TPT).

Everyone in our families can face harsh environments outside of the home. It doesn't matter if it is school, work, or even the grocery store. People and situations can be cruel. When we are at home together, it should not be another harsh environment. It should be a place full of the joy and love of God. An atmosphere like this doesn't just happen by accident. It takes purpose and effort on our part.

When I was growing up, my home was an extremely happy one. Looking back now, I realize it is because God's Word was our foundation. We had fun together; we laughed together. There were four kids, so of course, there were squabbles, but as a whole, it was a peaceful, joyful atmosphere.

My parents both worked at making it a place full of joy. My dad especially is a huge cut up, so aside from the spiritual aspect, he was always doing something to make us laugh.

One of my dad's favorite ways to make us laugh is by tickling. I have so many memories of us all laughing either because we were being tickled or we were laughing because we were watching someone else getting tickled. My mom is probably the most ticklish out of all of us, so she was usually his target. I can remember many times we would run to her "rescue" because she was being attacked.

My parents and I were laughing just the other day about a story that happened when I was about nine years old. My dad was chasing everyone around, tickling us and getting us to say something silly to get him to stop. Everyone would take all they could and then say whatever it was he had decided on. Then he got to me. Now, my daddy and I are extremely alike. He has told me before that I am him in a blonde wig. I can be extremely strong-willed, and I got that trait from my daddy. So, my dad kept tickling, and even though I had tears going down my face, I would not give in. He finally said, "Oh, you won't play the game right and gave up." To this day, I still claim I played the game right. I just won.

I have so many fun memories of us laughing together, and I am now blessed to be making so many memories full of laughter with my husband and children. Both of our boys definitely take after their papa in this department, and I am so glad.

Laughter is such a needed but sometimes overlooked thing. Sometimes between the dirty dishes, homework, sports practice, job responsibilities, running errands, and just life in general, it can be easy to get so busy that we don't take time to laugh together. Make time for that! We need to prioritize laughing with our family.

Our children need to see us laughing and having a good time. A miserable Mama makes for a miserable atmosphere at home. A joyful, peaceful Mama is what our families need us to be. They do not need us to be perfect, but they do need us to be full of joy. The only way we will ever be full of joy is through our ongoing, living connection with Jesus.

Mama, How to Be Truly Fulfilled

The truth is, Mama, we can get to our goal weight, go on the most exciting vacations, have the most amazing house, throw the most perfect events, and get all the best promotions at work. Really, we can achieve everything in life we could ever "want," but outside of Jesus, we will never be fulfilled. There is nothing in the world that can ever fulfill or satisfy us like Jesus can.

Society and social media have told us so many lies. That being a certain shape or size will satisfy, that a successful career will satisfy, that being in a relationship will satisfy, or having the right house or car will satisfy, but none of that will. These ideas leave so many constantly grasping for the next great thing, and every time they reach it, they find themselves unsatisfied again, so they are off after the next thing. But, Mama, we know the truth, so let's stop allowing this deception to have any hold in our lives!

> Jesus answered, "If you drink from Jacob's well you'll be thirsty again and again, but if anyone drinks the living water I give them, they will be forever satisfied! For when you drink the water I give you it becomes a gushing fountain of the Holy Spirit, springing up and flooding you with endless life!"
>
> John 4:13-14 (TPT)

Mama, we will never be happy apart from Jesus. The only way we will ever truly be fulfilled is to walk in all God has called us to do. God has specifically designed and created us for a purpose. If we are not doing what we are created for, we will not be fulfilled. We will never be completely fulfilled until we are fulfilling all that God has called us to do.

Like we talked about earlier, each of our lives and callings looks different, but there are some things all Mamas are called to do. We are all called to honor and obey God's Word. God will never call us to do anything that does not line up with His Word. If it is in the Word, we are to obey it. Obeying God always gets us in on His best!

"If you have a willing heart to let me help you, and if you will obey me, you will feast on the blessings of abundant harvest" (Isaiah 1:19, TPT).

"Yes,' said Jesus. 'But God will bless all who listen to the word of God and carefully obey everything they hear'" (Luke 11:28, TPT).

Knowing God's Word is great. Being in a church that preaches the uncompromised Word of God is amazing! We might even be able to quote a huge number of scriptures, but just knowing what God's Word says is not enough. We have to obey it. God's Word is the foundation to a successful life. But we only get that foundation by obeying His Word.

These words I speak to you are not incidental additions to your life, homeowner improvements to your standard of living. They are foundational words, words to build a life on. If you work these words into your life, you are like a smart carpenter who built his house on solid rock. Rain poured down, the river flooded, a tornado hit—but nothing moved that house. It was fixed to the rock. But if you just use my words in Bible studies and don't work them into your life, you are like a stupid carpenter who built his house on the sandy beach. When a storm rolled in and the waves came up, it collapsed like a house of cards.

Matthew 7:24-27 (MSG)

We are responsible for obeying the Word we hear. If we ever refuse to obey the Word we know, the Bible makes it clear we are deceiving ourselves. The devil doesn't even have to deceive us at that point. We are doing it ourselves. Deception never leads to fulfillment. It will only ever lead to destruction. No matter how big or how small it may seem, if it is God's Word, we should obey it.

Do what God's teaching says; don't just listen and do nothing. When you only sit and listen, you are fooling yourselves. Hearing God's teaching and doing nothing is like looking at your face in the mirror and doing nothing about you saw. You go away and immediately forget how bad you looked.

James 1:22-24 (ERV)

Don't fool yourself into thinking that you are a listener when you are anything but, letting the Word go in one ear and out the other. Act on what you hear! Those who hear and don't act are like those who glance in the mirror, walk away, and two minutes later have no idea who they are, what they look like.

James 1:22-24 (MSG)

True fulfillment only comes when we are following God's Word in every area of our lives. The Bible shows us this clearly.

"Respect the Lord and you will have a good life, one that is satisfying and free from trouble" (Proverbs 19:23, ERV).

"When you live a life of abandoned love, surrendered before the awe of God, here's what you'll experience: Abundant life. Continual protection. And complete satisfaction!" (Proverbs 19:23, TPT)

"Reverence for the Eternal leads to a fulfilled life; those who have it will sleep well, for disaster will not touch them" (Proverbs 19:23, VOICE).

Being where God has called us to be and doing what God has called us to do is where we will always find true satisfaction and fulfillment.

One of the best gifts we can give our families is a Mama that is fulfilled. A fulfilled Mama is a happy Mama. If we aren't happy and fulfilled, our families know it. Our families are also going to know when they have a Mama walking in her calling, totally fulfilled through her relationship with Jesus. That makes all the difference.

Mama, Recognize the *Real Enemy*

One key to being the happy Mama God designed us to be is to see our real enemy for who he is. Our enemy is not our kids, our husband, our in-laws, our never-ending to-do list, or our lack of sleep. The bottom line is, no matter the circumstances, our enemy is the devil, pure and simple. God's Word makes this very clear.

"For we are not fighting against human beings but against the wicked spiritual forces in the heavenly world, the rulers, authorities, and cosmic powers of this dark age" (Ephesians 6:12, GNT).

Our enemy is always the devil and his influence. When we let the Word of God open our eyes to this, then we know who and how to fight.

"Control yourselves and be careful! The devil is your enemy, and he goes around like a roaring lion looking for someone to attack and eat" (1 Peter 5:8, ERV).

"Most importantly, be disciplined and stay on guard. Your enemy the devil is prowling around outside like a roaring lion, just waiting and hoping for the chance to devour someone" (1 Peter 5:8, VOICE).

Whenever we let circumstances drive us into a "Mama melt-down," we are basically just swinging punches at everyone around but never hitting the real enemy. I don't mean swinging literal punches but verbal ones. Lashing out at our husband, snapping at our children, or even the harsh dialogue we sometimes have with ourselves. We are frustrated and are on the defense, but we are fighting the wrong ones. Our family is our God-given team, our support system. Our enemy is the devil. He is the one we should be going after.

If we Mamas let God open our eyes to the real enemy and go after him with the Word of God and our God-given authority, no demon in hell can stand in our family's way.

There is nothing more intense than a "Mama bear" going after whoever has messed with her family. I've never been between a Mama bear and her cub, and I never want to be. Let's go "Mama bear" on the devil if he tries to touch any of our loved ones. When we Mamas start going after the devil like we are called to, things will change in our families.

Will problems come? Absolutely. But no matter what is going on around us, we have the greater One living in us, and He causes us to always come out victorious!

"The Spirit who lives in you is greater than the spirit who lives in the world" (1 John 4:4, NLT).

"Yet even in the midst of all these things, we triumph over them all, for God has made us to be more than conquerors, and his demonstrated love is our glorious victory over everything!" (Romans 8:37, TPT)

We cannot just put up with the devil. There should be no tolerating him when he is harassing our families. His goal is always to steal, kill, and destroy our family. This isn't something we have to guess about. The Bible clearly lays it out for us.

"The thief comes with the sole intention of stealing and killing and destroying" (John 10:10, Phillips).

The same way that God only wants good things for your family, the devil only wants bad. He hates God, and he hates the family because God designed it. He especially hates a family full of the Word and on fire for God because a family like that can do a lot of damage to his kingdom.

Like I said earlier, if you ever have an attack against your family, see it for what it really is. Use your God-given authority and take care of business. Another way to keep the enemy out is to be on guard by watching what you allow in your home.

The devil is sneaky in the ways he tries to get in our homes. He is a master liar and deceiver. He is constantly looking for ways in, but he disguises them. He tries to make things look innocent a lot of times in the form of entertainment, so we will unknowingly give him an open door into our home.

Am I saying all entertainment is bad, and we should all throw out our TVs and streaming devices? Of course not! I'm just saying we need to be selective in what we let in our house. After all, what we allow in our eyes and ears will always come out.

"For the overflow of what has been stored in your heart will be seen by your fruit and will be heard in your words" (Luke 6:45, TPT).

Are we seeing attitudes or hearing language from our children that we don't like? We might as well be totally honest. Is there constant strife and arguing in the home? Does our household seem full of constant fear, anxiety, or unrest? Then we have to take a really good look at what our family is letting into our home.

Television shows, movies, and music that are full of bad language and ungodly lifestyles should not have any place in our homes. These things may seem small and unimportant, but that is the point of the devil's deception. It gets us to let our guard down and gives him open the door to get his foothold into our homes. He is sneaky and will take any little way in that he can.

"Guard your heart above all else, for it determines the course of your life" (Proverbs 4:23, NLT).

We have taught this scripture to our children from the time they were little. There are just certain things we do not watch or listen to in our house. John Parker is old enough to understand that it is because we are protecting our hearts.

One day close to a year ago, I was doing dishes in the kitchen, and John Parker was watching a show in the living room while Ezra was napping. I turned to check on John Parker at one point, and he was staring at the TV with this really upset look on his face. He had both hands holding his stomach. At first, I thought maybe he was hurting. When I asked him what was wrong, he answered very matter-of-factly, "There is a bad commercial on, and I am protecting my spirit!"

He didn't quite have the technique down, but his heart was so pure. That day was an awesome opportunity to teach him that things get in our hearts through our eyes and our ears. Now, if a commercial comes on he doesn't want in his heart, he closes his eyes and covers his ears. It is absolutely precious to watch our children start walking in the Word we have taught them. What we teach and impart into our family on a daily basis really does matter.

On a side note, if we tell our children to protect their hearts, but we watch and listen to whatever we want, they will not follow our instructions. If we do not see the value in protecting our hearts, our children will not see the value in protecting theirs. "Do as I say, not as I do" never works.

Following God's Word is for every part of our lives. No part is exempt. There is no area where compromise is okay. God's Word was never meant to just be reserved for Sundays at church. That is a very believable deception from our enemy. It is extremely crucial to the future of our families that we follow the Holy Spirit every day of our lives in every area of our lives!

"If we are living now by the Holy Spirit's power, let us follow the Holy Spirit's leading in every part of our lives" (Galatians 5:25, TLB).

Mama, I encourage you strongly to trust the leading of the Holy Spirit. If we do not have peace with something, it is so important that we follow the Spirit's leading. If a television show, movie, book, or song doesn't sit right with us, we do not have to let it in our homes. Even if it seems our children are the only ones missing out. If we are honoring God, we are never missing out. It is vital we always follow what God puts on our hearts and let His peace lead us.

"Let your heart be always guided by the peace of the Anointed One" (Colossians 3:15, TPT).

In Greek, it literally means "let peace be the umpire of your minds." What does an umpire do in a baseball game? They tell who is safe and who is unsafe. Let God's peace do the same in your life by telling you what is safe and what is not. Trust that you hear God's voice and be quick to follow His leading.

"My own sheep will hear my voice and I know each one, and they will follow me" (John 10:27, TPT).

For far too long, the devil has wreaked havoc in our homes. For far too long, our homes have been filled with strife, stress, complaining, and division. But I am asking you today to stand up with me and say, "Enough is enough!" Let's take our God-given authority, use the name of Jesus, and kick the devil out of our families. Let's get him out of our houses and put him back where he belongs—under our feet!

Mama, Stop Allowing Emotions to Call the Shots

∞∞∞∞∞∞∞∞∞∞

Sometimes it seems like I can go through more emotions in fifteen minutes than my husband does in an entire week. I'm sure I could get a big "Amen" from him right now! Can any Mamas relate to me on this one?

Personally, I tend to be a crier. I cry at almost everything. If I'm happy, sad, frustrated, laughing, tired, whatever it is, I usually cry. Not sobbing, but I get choked up. The other day I cried at a sweet television commercial I saw and then cried again when I tried to tell Jeremiah about it later. I usually blame the crying on leftover pregnancy hormones, but the reality is I was like this long before either pregnancy. It's just part of who I am. I used to get really frustrated and embarrassed over it, but the Lord has shown me that having a tender heart is in no way a bad thing.

Women tend to be emotional creatures, and there is nothing wrong with that! God made us that way. Emotions are not bad things. God is the one who designed emotions. He gave them to us. The key is He created them to enhance our life, never to control it.

Our emotions make a very poor leader. They are just so fickle. They can be up one day and down the next or can sometimes change from minute to minute. God's Word and way of doing things never change. His Word, not our emotions, is supposed to determine our steps in life.

"Your Word is a lamp to my feet and a light to my path" (Psalm 119:105, AMP).

"Your Word is like a lamp for my feet and a light for my path [it shows how life should be lived]" (Psalm 119:105, EXB).

God's Word makes a much better gauge for our life than our emotions do. Our emotions can be influenced by anything and everything. If we let our emotions control us, we will be all over the place.

All too often, we let how we feel at the moment dictate how we interact with everyone around us. We feel stressed or frustrated, so we lash out at our family. We feel tired, so our once long fuse seems shorter and quicker to spark. We feel sad or hurt, so we pout or distance ourselves to let everyone know it. I could keep going with examples, but whatever emotions we are feeling, even if they are "justified," we cannot let them affect how we treat those around us.

"If you live without restraint and are unable to control your temper, you are as helpless as a city with broken down defenses, open to attack" (Proverbs 25:28, TPT).

"Patience is better than power, and controlling one's emotions, than capturing a city" (Proverbs 16:32, CSB).

If we let our emotions lead us, we end up creating an atmosphere that is turbulent and only produces instability. But, if we let God's Word lead us and walk by faith instead of emotions, our lives and homes become an atmosphere in which God can work. When our homes are a place where God can work, the results are worth it!

Whenever we let our emotions lead us instead of God's Word, we have given our emotions, not Jesus, the place of Lord in our life. Lord is defined as "someone or something having power, authority or influence." If we let our emotions control us, we have made our emotions Lord. Jesus cannot work somewhere if He isn't allowed to lead.

"What good does it do for you to say I am your Lord and Master if what I teach you is not put into practice?" (Luke 6:46, TPT).

"But don't let the passion of your emotions lead you to sin! Don't let anger control you or be fuel for revenge, not for even a day. Don't give the slanderous accuser, the Devil, an opportunity to manipulate you!" (Ephesians 4:26-27, TPT).

The Bible makes it very clear in this passage that Satan will try to use our emotions to manipulate us. These verses are God giving us a "heads up" so we will know what to be on guard against.

One of the biggest biblical examples of a Mama that didn't let her emotions dictate her actions is the woman in 2 Kings 4:8-37. I encourage you to read her story, but for now, I'm just going to sum it up.

The Bible doesn't tell us many details about her. It tells us that she was from Shunem, she and her husband were very rich, her husband was old, and they didn't have any children. But even with such few details, her story is so powerful.

She loved God and honored His prophet. Every time Elisha came through town, she and her husband would feed him. Eventually, she asked her husband to build a room for the prophet, so he would have a place to stay.

Because of her honor for God and his prophet Elisha, God blessed her. He gave her the one thing she didn't have, a son. Elisha gave her a Word from the Lord, saying, "Next year this time you will be holding a son in your arms." And a year later, she had her son.

The next verses pick up some years later when her son is older. He is out in the field with his father, and he complains about his head hurting. His father sends him into the house with his mother because everyone needs their Mama when they are hurting. Then the Bible tells us in 2 Kings 4:20 (VOICE), "And about noon, while the boy was sitting in his mother's lap, he died."

Sometimes I think we read things in the Bible, and if we are not careful, we kind of gloss over what we read. Stop and really think about that verse for just a minute. It is not just a story. It really happened.

This is a real woman, a real Mama that had her son die in her arms. Can you imagine with me for just a minute the strong flood of emotions that she experienced? Devastation, pain, loss, panic, overwhelming sadness. Really beyond what anyone can comprehend if they haven't experienced it. I'm sure her emotions tried to completely overwhelm her, but she did not let her emotions dictate her actions!

The next couple of verses go on to tell us she lays her son's body on the prophet's bed and goes to get Elisha. God had promised her a son, and she was not letting her circumstances steal that promise from her. She let her faith in God's promise, not her emotions, control her actions. She did not let anything move her. Then as you read further, her son is miraculously raised! She experienced a miracle in her family! Her son was raised from the dead! All because of this, Mama refused to let her emotions call the shots.

In Kellie Copeland's book, *Protecting Your Family in Dangerous Times*, she shares an absolutely powerful testimony about a time where her family experienced a miracle because she refused to let her emotions sway her. (If you have not read her book, I strongly encourage you to read it. If you have read it, I strongly encourage you to read it again. It is a priceless weapon in a Mama's spiritual arsenal.)

She tells about one Christmas years ago when her children were small, and one of her daughters became very sick. They took her to the hospital, and she was diagnosed with meningitis. The doctors told them she would possibly not make it through the night. At that time, many children had died of meningitis in their area, some in that same hospital. As a Mama, hearing such a terrible report about one of her children wasn't easy. Her emotions tried to go wild. Fear tried to take over, but she did not allow that! Kellie turned to her sister and said, "I refuse to fear!" She did not let her emotions control how she acted in that situation. She stood on the Word of God, and her daughter experienced a supernatural recovery!

These are just two examples of Mamas that did not let their emotions control how they responded in situations. By faith, they stood on what God's Word said, and because of that, they saw God move in their children. Our situation may not seem that dire, but every day we do face situations that give us the opportunity to either succumb to our emotions or walk by faith in God's Word.

"For we walk by faith, not by sight [living our lives in a manner consistent with our confident belief in God's promises]" (2 Corinthians 5:7, AMP).

"The path we walk is charted by faith, not by what we see with our eyes" (2 Corinthians 5:7, VOICE).

When the Bible tells us to "walk by faith," it means in every area of our life. No part of our life is exempt. We are people of faith. We are Mamas of faith. Faith is our way of life. Nothing changes that.

As you know, we have two boys. They are currently five and two. For any Mamas who haven't had boys, let me describe it to you a little. Boys are wild. They are pretty wide open, daring, and full of adventure. We have never dealt with anything life-threatening, but them being so full of energy and lack of inhibition has caused some situations that have tried to bring fear.

Once when John Parker was about three years old, I had gone down the hall to change clothes for church. Jeremiah was still at work, so I was trying to get us both ready in a hurry to meet him at service. Our house is "baby proof," so leaving the room for a minute seemed fine in theory. I wasn't gone very long, and I left the bedroom door open so I could listen to him. All of a sudden, I heard a loud crash and horribly painful screams. I ran down the hallway to discover that he had somehow completely pulled a drawer out of our entertainment center, and it had fallen on his right foot. This drawer was extremely heavy. It was solid wood, filled with movies, and had fallen from a couple of feet off the ground. As soon as I moved the drawer, I could tell his foot was already swollen and turning colors. He was in extreme pain and couldn't put any weight on it, so I scooped him up and immediately began speaking the Word.

Everything inside of me wanted to panic, but what good would that have done John Parker? I refused to let my emotions control my reaction. Because I had taken time to fill my heart with the Word of God beforehand, it was stored inside of me, ready to come out. I only let God's Word come out of my mouth and gave God open the door to work a miracle. Within just a few minutes, John Parker's foot was completely healed. He was completely pain-free and had no proof of the previous injury!

Between the two boys, Ezra has probably given us more opportunities to panic or freak out. He runs ninety to nothing constantly, usually not looking where he is going, and he loves to climb. He is also quiet and quick to figure things out, so he really keeps us on our toes. Jeremiah says that when we get to heaven, we will know which angels were Ezra's because they will be the ones lying down in the corner breathing heavily since they are finally getting a break! Our house was "baby proof" with John Parker; now it is more than "baby proof"—it is "Ezra proof."

Once when he was a little under a year old, I was folding laundry in the living room where the boys were playing and watching a movie. Ezra decided to climb the couch for the first time, and thankfully I was right there. Instead of sitting down next to his brother, he immediately jumped and dove head-first off the couch. My "Momma reflexes" kicked in, and I caught him by one foot with his head barely a couple of inches from our hardwood floor! Before I even had time to set him down, he excitedly exclaimed, "Whoa! Fun!" Let me tell you, that boy has given me many, many opportunities to test and see if I would let my emotions react or my faith.

It is vital that we Mamas stay so full of the Word and in such close fellowship with God that when our emotions start trying to take over, we can recognize them. They may possibly be very validated emotions, but they are not our controlling factor. We have authority over our emotions; they do not have authority over us unless we let them.

When our emotions seem like they are going haywire, let's take a minute. Take a step back, pray in the Spirit, and get our focus back on God's Word. Doing these things are key to us talking and acting in a way that opens the door for God to work in our homes. And like the stories earlier show us, when we create an atmosphere that allows for God to work, miracles happen!

Mama, Watch Your Mouth

This chapter and the previous chapter really go hand in hand. Our emotions and our words are so closely linked because most of the time, we are used to just saying whatever we feel. That seems normal because that is what everyone around us does, but that is not God's normal. Since we are Word Mamas, our normal should be God's normal, not anyone else's.

As we discussed earlier, we Mamas really have a lot of influence over what goes on in our home. If we are constantly grumpy, murmuring, and complaining, our family will be too. Our children imitate us. If we are stressed out and on edge, the atmosphere we create will influence our family to be the same.

Mama, watch your mouth! Even if our emotions seem to be going wild and we feel hurt, scared, sad, or frustrated, we do not have to speak it! What we say determines whether we open the door for God to work in our family or open the door for the devil to work in our family.

"And we must not embrace their ways by complaining— grumbling with discontent, as many of them did, and were killed by the destroyer!" (1 Corinthians 10:10, TPT)

The Bible makes it very clear that our words have power. That is a spiritual truth. What we say really matters.

"Your words are so powerful that they will kill or give life" (Proverbs 18:21, TPT).

"Words kill, words give life; they're either poison or fruit—you choose" (Proverbs 18:21, MSG).

Even beyond the spiritual aspect of it, no one enjoys being around someone that is always negative and complaining. Anyone like that is just simply no fun to be around. Someone that is always letting everyone know how miserable they are will make everyone else around them miserable too.

Have you ever been around someone who seemed to suck the fun out of any room? Let's not be that person. Mama, we should not be doing that in our homes.

"You would be better off living in the middle of the desert than with an angry and argumentative wife" (Proverbs 21:19, VOICE).

"A constant dripping on a rainy day and a wife's bickering are very much alike" (Proverbs 27:15, VOICE).

"An endless drip, drip, drip from a leaky faucet and the words of a cranky, nagging wife have the same effect" (Proverbs 27:15, TPT).

"A nagging wife can drive you crazy!" (Proverbs 19:13, TPT)

I really don't know why the author of Proverbs seemed to write so much about a nagging wife. My guess is because Solomon is the author, and he had three hundred wives! I'm sure he experienced his fair share of nagging. I know this seems like the women are getting picked on, and I know we could all think, *Well, my husband does that too.* I'm not arguing that but this book is to Mamas, so I'm not writing to the men. This book is just for us girls.

In the spirit of being totally honest, this is something I am still really working on. I am a perfectionist. I have been often referred to as an overachiever. I have always held myself to an extremely high standard. I tend to be pretty hard on myself, and if I don't let the Holy Spirit keep me in check, I can be hard on everyone around me without even meaning to be. Just because that's how I am at times does not mean it is okay.

Life happens. Things don't always go the way we plan, especially with kids. We cannot always control every detail, but we can always control how we react. Just the other day, I had an opportunity to get frustrated or be critical of my husband, but thanks to the Lord, I did not.

A couple of nights ago, I was making a quiche for dinner. It is a favorite around this house. I can get both of our boys to eat it without any issues, so it is an amazing "go-to." I was in a hurry that night and running behind, so instead of making the crust like I usually do, I went against everything inside of me and decided to save time and go with store-bought. I texted my husband Jeremiah and asked if he could pick up a pie crust on the way home.

Let me give you a little backstory with this. He is always so great to make store runs for me in a pinch, but it has kind of turned into a running joke between us that he usually buys the wrong thing. He is sweet to help but cannot seem to find the right item at the grocery store to save his life. If he ever has to go to the store, I write him an extremely detailed list so he cannot accidentally get the wrong thing. But the other night, I was in a hurry and just texted to ask for a pie crust because I didn't think that could get messed up. Well, I was wrong.

A little while later, Jeremiah came home with a grocery bag. He set it down on the counter while the boys were basically tackling him with hugs. As they pulled him into the toy room to play, I opened the bag to pour my quiche mixture in. The pie crust in the bag was a graham cracker crust. All of a sudden, the perfect dinner I had planned would not be perfect anymore. Now, this might sound silly to you, but to a Southern girl like me, anything in the kitchen is serious business. At first, I was frustrated. I could have griped, complained, and criticized, but I didn't. I took a minute and prayed in the Spirit before I said anything. I gave the Holy Spirit a chance to influence my reaction instead of just running my mouth. I laughed, thanked Jeremiah for running by the store, and then announced dinner would be low carb. That night things didn't go perfectly, and for a perfectionist, that is a huge deal, but what good would it do for me to put my husband down? He made an honest mistake. He was trying to be helpful.

Being hard or critical on our loved ones is not helping them. When we speak to our families, words filled with love and encouragement will make the difference. This applies even when we are disciplining our children. We should never discipline or correct out of anger. We should always do it out of love, just like the Lord does with us. After all, He is in us, ready to help us in every area of our lives.

"And never let ugly or hateful words come from your mouth, but instead let your words become beautiful gifts that encourage others; do this by speaking words of grace to help them" (Ephesians 4:29, TPT).

I love that this translation uses the word "ugly" as one of the words to describe what should not be coming out of our mouths. If you are from the South, I'm pretty positive you know what the phrase "acting/being ugly" means. It is acting in a way that is not nice or becoming. Maybe most everyone knows that phrase, but my husband, who was born and raised in Minnesota, had never heard it until we were married.

One day, just a few weeks after our wedding, we ran by the bank together. My sister, Sarah, worked there at the time, so we went inside to see her. As we were walking in, Sarah was waiting on a customer, and this lady was extremely rude. After she walked out, I whispered to Jeremiah, "That lady was so ugly!" The look of shock on his face was priceless. "What?" he said, completely appalled his wife would say something that rude about someone. "You can't say that about people." Without yet understanding my southern colloquialism had been lost in translation, I replied, "Why not? She was being ugly." The shock on his face was replaced by confusion. "Wait, being ugly?" That day I explained the southern saying of "being/ acting ugly." That wasn't the first time I had to explain a Southern saying to him, and it definitely wasn't the last.

I really like that phrase because I feel like it captures it so well. Rude, critical, and harsh words are not beautiful words. They are ugly and hurtful. The verse earlier explains that our words should be ones that build up our family, not tear them down. What and how we talk to our family matters.

> I may speak in different languages, whether human or even angels. But if I don't have love, I am only a noisy bell or a ringing cymbal. I may have the gift of prophecy, I may understand all secrets and know everything there is to know, and I may have faith so great I can move mountains. But even with all this, if I don't have love, I am nothing. I may give away everything I have to help others, and I may even

give my body as an offering to be burned. But I gain nothing by doing all this if I don't have love.

1 Corinthians 13:1-3 (ERV)

We could even be telling our families the right things, but if it is said outside of love, it is doing more harm than good. God never corrects or teaches us outside of love. It is imperative for our families that we follow His example.

"Nothing is more appealing than speaking beautiful, life-giving words. For they release sweetness to our souls and inner healing to our spirits" (Proverbs 16: 24, TPT).

"Kind words are like honey; they are easy to accept and good for your health" (Proverbs 16:24, ERV)

"Kind words heal and help; cutting words wound and maim" (Proverbs 15:4, MSG).

"Gentle words cause life and health; griping brings discouragement" (Proverbs 15:4, TLB)

It is vital to us that we remember if we are harsh or critical to others, it is hurting them, but we are hurting ourselves as well.

"When you're kind to others, you help yourself; when you're cruel to others, you hurt yourself" (Proverbs 11:17, MSG).

It is vital for us and our families that we watch our mouths. Speaking kind, God-filled words to our family affects everyone drastically different than if we are speaking harsh, criticism-filled words.

"He who guards his mouth and his tongue keeps himself from troubles" (Proverbs 21:23, AMPC).

"Watch your words and be careful what you say, and you'll be surprised how few troubles you'll have" (Proverbs 21:23, TPT).

The scripture says, "If you want to enjoy true life and have only good days, then avoid saying anything hurtful" (1 Peter 3:10, ERV).

Like any other commandment in the Bible, that can sound like an extremely tall order. It can seem pretty much impossible to change the way we talk, but just like any other commandment in the Bible, God never intended for us to do it on our own. He gave us His Holy Spirit to be our helper in everything (John 14:15), and He empowers us to do all that we are commanded to do.

"Help me to guard my words whenever I say something" (Psalm 141:3, CEV).

"Lord, help me control my tongue; help me be careful about what I say" (Psalm 141:3, NCV).

That is my daily prayer, and today I encourage you to make this your prayer too! I know circumstances can be harsh at times, but our words do not have to be. In every single situation, we get to choose how we will speak and react.

I am in no way claiming to have this down. I don't always handle every situation perfectly. None of us do, but we are always learning and growing. And oh, the Lord can do such great things with just a willing heart!

Mama, Do Not Compare
What God Has Prepared

◇◇◇◇◇◇◇◇◇◇◇◇◇

"Comparison is the thief of joy" (Theodore Roosevelt).

That quotation is absolutely spot on. One of the major tools the devil uses to steal our joy and make us Mamas unhappy is comparison. Comparison is a horrible, vicious cycle designed by Satan himself. Comparison will lead to discouragement, jealousy, strife, tension, resentment, and division. None of those are the traits of a happy Mama.

Comparison only opens the door to envy, resentment, and jealousy, and they bring nothing but destruction. Comparison brings nothing but an evil outcome because it originated with the devil himself.

"I will make myself like the Most High" (Isaiah 14:14, AMP).

He already had an amazing call. He was Lucifer, the angel in charge of all of the worship of heaven. He had such a beautiful anointing, but comparison left him unsatisfied. Instead of focusing on his anointing and calling, he was consumed with wanting to be like God. He wanted God's position. He destroyed himself, trying to be God. Our situations might not seem as drastic, but, in the same way, we will destroy ourselves if we try to be someone else.

"For wherever you find jealousy and rivalry you also find disharmony and all other kinds of evil" (James 3:16, Phillips).

If you look around, comparison is absolutely everywhere. Even the magazines in the grocery store and articles online ask us, "Who wore it better?" The temptation to compare is always in our face.

Social media has so many great uses. It can be entertaining. It keeps us connected with our loved ones, but it can sadly make it easier than ever for us to get sucked into comparison. An opportunity to compare ourselves to someone else is never farther away from us than our cell phone.

The worst part about social media is that it gives us unrealistic standards and expectations. We only see what people want us to see. Am I the only Mama that has cleaned a spot in the house to take a picture? Someone else might see that post and think, *Wow, I wish my house was that clean!* Listen, not even my house is that clean. Just the spot I showed you was. Do you ever wish you looked like a girl in a magazine? She probably doesn't even look like that in real life.

Comparison has sadly turned many God-given friends into enemies. People placed in our lives by God to love us, stretch us, and grow us have been pushed out of our lives because of comparison. It has turned beautiful relationships ugly. It pits people against each other. Nothing good comes out of comparison.

Comparison is a never-ending cycle. There will always be someone who seems to have it better than us, someone who seems to have more, or someone who seems to be farther ahead in life.

One day while I was doing things around the house, God spoke to me. I don't remember exactly what I was doing, but it was probably laundry because I am pretty much always folding laundry. Whatever I was doing, the Lord spoke to me. He said, "Don't compare what I have prepared."

We have to stop comparing what God has prepared for us to what God has prepared for someone else. God is good, and His Word tells us He has good plans for each of us. None of us are left out.

"I know what I'm doing. I have it all planned out—plans to take care of you, not abandon you, plans to give you a future you hope for" (Jeremiah 29:11, MSG).

"'For I know the plans I have for you,' says the Eternal, 'Plans for peace, not evil, to give you a future and hope— never forget that'" (Jeremiah 29:11, VOICE).

If we keep our focus on the good plans God has for us instead of comparing our life to someone else's, we will find ourselves much more content and at peace. As we discussed earlier, true fulfillment comes from walking in God's plan for us.

We are all different, all special, all unique. All of our callings are different, and each one is needed. There is nothing to compare ourselves to because I was not made to be you, just as you were not made to be me. If we are busy trying to be like someone else, we are going to be miserable, and our callings will be left unfulfilled.

A good example of this would be driving a car. What happens if we are driving and get distracted by something on the side of the road? If whatever keeps our attention too long, we can end up in a wreck. The same thing can happen in our lives if we are stuck in the never-ending cycle of comparison. We can get so busy keeping our eyes on what others have and are doing that we lose sight of where we are going. With our eyes on others instead of Jesus, our lives can end up miserably wrecked.

No one else can be you as well as you can. In the same way, you cannot be anyone else as well as you can be you. Stop trying to be like anyone else! You will never succeed at that. Be you God created you to be!

> So, since we find ourselves fashioned into all these excellently formed and marvelously functioning parts in Christ's body, let's just go ahead and be what we were made to be, without enviously or pridefully comparing ourselves with each other, or trying to be something we aren't.
>
> Romans 12:6 (MSG)

We are Word Mamas. Our normal doesn't look like the rest of the world's normal. Just because comparison seems to be going on everywhere around us does not mean it should be part of our lives.

> And here's why: you are still living in the flesh, not in the Spirit. How do I know? Are you fighting with one another? Are you comparing yourselves to others and becoming consumes with jealousy? Then it sounds like you are living in the flesh, no different from the rest who live by the standards of this rebellious and broken world.
>
> 1 Corinthians 3:3 (VOICE)

> For you are living your lives dominated by the mind-set of the flesh. Ask yourselves, "Is there jealousy among you?" Do you compare yourselves with others? Do you quarrel like children and end up taking sides? If so, this proves that you are living your lives centered on yourselves, dominated by the mind-set of the flesh, and behaving like unbelievers.
>
> 1 Corinthians 3:3 (TPT)

That means we will not compare ourselves with each other as if one of us were better and another worse. We have far more interesting things to do with our lives. Each of us is an original.

Galatians 5:26 (MSG)

So may we never be arrogant, or look down on another, for each of us is an original. We must forsake all jealousy that diminishes the value of others.

Galatians 5:26 (TPT)

There seems to be so much comparison and strife amongst women. Men are not exempt, but it seems to be amplified amongst us. It is because the devil knows what happens when there is unity. Unity leaves no door open for him to work. When we women stand arm in arm, in support of each other, completely unified in God, he knows we cannot be stopped, and that terrifies him.

We Mamas need to be each other's biggest cheerleaders. Cheering each other on and pushing each other forward in life. Lifting up, never putting down. When we are secure and confident in whom God has created us to be, we do not have to compare ourselves to anyone else. We can be happy for other's achievements because we know God has great things planned for us as well.

The only thing we should ever compare our life to is the Word of God. We should constantly be looking into the Word to see how our life compares to it. If our life doesn't line up with the Word, that is when we should make changes, but we should never change our lives to look like someone else's.

Mama, Let's Set the Atmosphere

◇◇◇◇◇◇◇◇◇◇◇◇◇

As we are closing out this book, I want to give you some practical ways to set the atmosphere in your home. I cannot take credit for any of these. They are all ideas that the Lord has given us for our family. He is so good like that.

1. Spend Time in God's Word every day.

Like we talked about in chapter four, we cannot give our family something we do not have. We cannot fill our homes with an atmosphere full of God if we have not first cultivated that atmosphere inside of us.

We have to make our time with Jesus every day more vital than our first cup of coffee. Do any other Mamas feel me on this one? The first thing I do every morning is to grab my Bible, my notebook, and my cup of coffee. I call it my morning coffee date with Jesus, and I absolutely adore it! I look forward to that special time alone with Him every day.

Will we always feel like spending our time with Jesus? No. There will be days we feel too tired. There will be days we feel too busy. But, if we realize the value of it, we will spend time with Him anyway.

2. Keep the Word and/or worship music going in our home constantly.

With everything else we and our families deal with daily, it is vital that we find ways to get the Word in our hearts. We do that by putting it in our eyes and our ears. The world is constantly trying to fill our hearts with its junk, so we have to combat that with God's Word.

We are truly blessed to have so many platforms to keep the Word and faith-filled worship going in our homes. Let's take advantage of it.

God has given our family some ideas that we absolutely love on how to keep the Word in our home.

- If we are not watching TV, we have KCM's Victory Channel on. Even if we are sleeping or leaving the house, we keep it going.

- We worship together as a family every night before bed. It is a simple song that I grew up singing often with my family. Watching our children lift their hands every night and sing is the sweetest thing! Once we put Ezra in bed, we sing "Power in the Blood" with him. He loves going to sleep! John Parker will avoid bedtime at all cost, but not Ezra. If we are late getting him to bed, he starts heading to his room and loudly announces, "Power! Bed!" That is his way of telling us he wants in bed to sing "Power in the Blood."

- On the way to school, we make confessions with John Parker. We use the "Power Packed Confessions for Kids" from the *Women of the Word Scripture Prayer Handbook* that my mom wrote. They even have the confessions available in laminated form so you can keep it in the car. It is a great way to get the Word in your children and you on the way to school.

- We read the Bible together as a family. Things can get hectic, but we make time for it. Our kids can seem distracted once their attention spans run out, but we still read. The Word is still getting into their hearts.
- Every morning when our boys first ask to watch television, we always have them watch something that feeds their Spirits. We are teaching them that feeding our spirits always comes first. "Commander Kellie and The Superkids" is a favorite in our house. Each one is fun and also packed so full of the Word.

3. Get in the church God has called you to. Stay faithful and serve there.

Where we go to church really makes a huge difference for us and our families. Gloria Copeland said, "Where you go to church makes the difference in life and death." That is so true! When trials and tribulations come, the foundation we have really makes a difference. It is essential to our families' futures that we get in a church that teaches the uncompromised Word of God.

There are a lot of amazing churches out there preaching the Word, but we are not supposed to pick churches like we pick a new car. See what features work best for us and what style we prefer. We are supposed to decide where to go to church like we should decide anything else in our lives—by seeking God and following His leading. He has a specific church for each of us.

"This is where God comes in. God has meticulously put this body together; He placed each part in the exact place to perform the exact function He wanted" (1 Corinthians 12:18, VOICE).

God has a specific church for our family and a specific supply for each one of us to bring. The supply we bring to our church is just as vital as the supply our church brings to us. From the time our children are young, we should help them get involved in serving at church (Proverbs 22:6).

4. Pray together as a family.

Prayer is communicating with God, and like in any other relationship, communication is crucial. It is vital for us and each member of our family to have a thriving prayer life.

I strongly encourage you to get involved in prayer at your church, but prayer is not something reserved just for church. Our children need to be involved in prayer at home too. If our children only see us pray at church, they will not see the value in it because they do not see us value it.

We pray together as a family every night before bed. We also go to Intercessory Prayer at our church every Sunday morning at 8:30 a.m. Getting our whole family there can be hectic, and keeping our kids' attention during prayer can be even more hectic. There are honestly a lot of Sundays where I just think it would be easier to pray from home, but we know the value of having our children there.

Earlier today, I was changing Ezra's clothes, and he kept saying, "Bray. Bray. Church." I could not figure out what in the world he was saying. I was trying to guess who at church he wanted to see or what toy he wanted to play with in the nursery. After saying it probably ten times or more, he grabbed my hands and stuck them together and said, "I bray church." I finally got it. "Oh, you want to pray at church?" He so sweetly answered, "Sure!"

That moment made every crazy Sunday morning totally worth it.

5. Take communion together as a family.

This is something we do together as a family almost every night. We also do it with my parents and siblings on every holiday and sometimes just because we are together. Jesus said, "As often as you take this cup remember Me" (1 Corinthians 11:24-26). So, we do it often.

Taking communion isn't complicated or hard. God's Word lays it out clearly for us. You can even read directly out of the Bible while taking it (Matthew 26:26-28, Luke 22:19-20).

It is such a sacred, holy thing that we have been invited to do. The juice and the cracker do not turn into some "magic potion" when combined. The power behind Communion is that it gets our focus back on Jesus and His sacrifice. It gets us to remember what He paid for.

6. Be quick to repent and quick to forgive.

Will we all do everything perfectly every time? Of course not. We will all be learning and growing until the day we go to heaven. It is important that our children see us take responsibility and repent whenever we mess up. If Jeremiah or I act in a way we shouldn't, we go quickly to apologize to our children. It is not fun or easy. But if our children grow up watching us being quick to repent, they will be quick to repent as well.

Will our children do things right all the time? Of course not. They are learning and growing too. It is important that when they do mess up, we love and forgive them. That doesn't mean we don't correct them, that is part of loving them, but we should never put them down for messing up or hold it over their heads. If we are quick to forgive them, they will grow up being quick to forgive others.

This list isn't everything you can do, but it is a great starting point. Pray and ask the Lord for ideas that are perfect for your family. He is always faithful to give wisdom to whoever asks Him.

> If you don't have all the wisdom needed for this journey, then all you have to do is ask God for it; and God will grant all that you need. He gives lavishly and never scolds you for asking.
>
> James 1:5 (VOICE)

Every family is different. Every child is unique. Being a Mama might not come with an instruction manual, but it does come with the Instructor. God knows what each of our families needs. He wants to instruct us. He wants to lead us. He wants to guide us.

If you are married, you and your husband need to team up to set and protect the atmosphere in your home. If you are a single Mama, God has given you the strength and grace to do whatever is needed for your family. Pray and get the plan from God for your family. Remember, anything God tells you to do, He equips you and anoints you to do it!

I know that God has amazing plans for you and your family (Jeremiah 29:11). I strongly encourage you to let Him be involved in every area of your lives and watch all that God can do!

When you and your family are walking in all that God has for you, Mama will be happy. More so, Mama will be full of joy and totally fulfilled. And when Mama is, everyone else in the family will be too.

You and God have got this, Mama!

About the Author

◇◇◇◇◇◇◇◇◇◇◇◇◇

Averill Gardner Johnson comes from a rich heritage of preachers and Bible teachers. She enjoys writing and speaking about the awkward and sometimes downright embarrassing adventures that we all call "life." Every reader will be quickly fascinated by her escapades and find themselves brought to tears of laughter, which will shortly turn to head-nodding approval of the wisdom in lessons learned.

Averill tackled her first public speech at the age of three and continues today as a conference speaker and minister of the Gospel. She is a 2009 graduate of GO Ministries International. While there, she met her husband, Jeremiah, and now they are the happy parents of John Parker and Ezra. She and Jeremiah are ordained ministers. They are the youth pastors of their home church, and they enjoy traveling together to minister.

Averill can be followed on Facebook.com/Averill Gardner Johnson and Instagram @averillgardnerjohnson.

You can also write her at P.O. Box 2127 Jasper, AL 35502. Phone (205)221-1747.

CPSIA information can be obtained
at www.ICGtesting.com
Printed in the USA
LVHW052201230621
690929LV00015B/2386